This Book Belongs To

Cydv

Nerdel's ABC Book

Published by The Nerdel Company

Printed in U.S.A.

ISBN 9780982335727

Library of Congress Control Number: 2009925234

We would like to say thank you to a few special people in our lives that made this book possible:

A very special thank you to our daughter Alexis for listening to all of the stories and rhymes thousands of times and always making it seem like it was the very first time she had heard them. She is a most incredible and wonderful person and we are blessed to have her in our lives.

A special thank you to our most talented cartoonist, Ms. Natali Martinez for her amazing interpretations of our ideas and for bringing Nerdel to life.

We also want to express our thanks to Ms. Ninette Katsoulos, an amazing individual who has helped in the preparation of this book. Her persistence and ideas have helped shape this book and ones to follow.

A special thank you to Mrs. Shirlie Kesselman, a wonderful lady who has believed in Nerdel since his inception and who has always had confidence that this project will succeed.

Finally, we want to thank every parent, teacher, brother or sister, who reads this book to a child. Our children are our precious jewels and we need to empower them with the information they need to grow up healthy, happy and strong. Nerdel is here to help!!!

In loving memory of
Ruth and Bernhard Garfinkel
Loving and wonderful parents and grandparents.

Nerdel's ABC Book

a b c

Written by
Drs. Robin and Marc Kesselman
Illustrated by Natali Martinez

Nerdel says **A**pple begins with an **A**, I wish I could eat one everyday.

Benny says Berries and he hears a B - mix them all together in a big smoothie.

Bb

Carrots - Penny says "give me a C". They're good for your eyes and yummy as can be.

D is for Dairy. That's milk, yogurt and cheese. It builds strong bones with the greatest of ease.

Edamame can you say that with me.
Those are soy beans that start with an E.

Natasha says eat **F**iber
such as vegetables, fruits and grains.
That **F** keeps you moving
like a locomotive train.

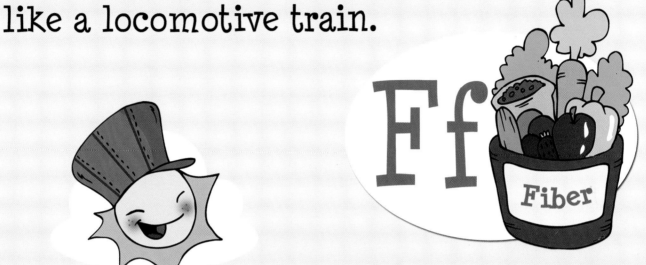

Nicki eats **G**rapes, they are super **G** - great. Purple, green and red, you don't need a plate.

Gg

Honey - an H that's sweet from bees. It sweetens up your oatmeal with a little squeeze.

Ices - begin with an I.
Fresh frozen fruit,
just give it a try.

Juice - drink this J in moderation. Mix it with water for a taste sensation.

Kiwi - Theo says K.
It's green and juicy, from
a land far away.

Lettuce - this L grows from the ground. It's great in salads and wraps, but it's not always round.

Milk - keep it low fat. It's good for your bones, but don't give it to the cat.

M m

Nuts - Natasha says they are nutritious, but Nerdel says this **N** is also delicious.

Olive Oil - It's double O good. A bread dipping treat, try some if you would.

Potatoes - start with a P. White, sweet, purple or gold, which one will it be?

Q - Quick, get on your feet.
Move around a little
and get off your seat.

Raspberries - an R that makes bakers happy. Baking with raspberries makes their tarts quite snappy.

Salmon - This S is smart.
Eating lots of fish is good for
your heart.

S s

Smart SALMON

Tomato - a shiny red T,
it's really a fruit that's
healthy as can be.

U - Understand
"The New Nerdel Way".
Put fitness and nutrition
on your red carpet today.

Veggies - There are so many to choose. Nicki says, "if you eat veggies you just can't lose."

Water - We hear a **W**.
It's the best drink of
all, for me and for you.

X -Be eXtra careful each day, what you eat at school and what you eat at play.

eXtra careful
Xx

Make the right choices

Y- Y stands for **you**.
You make the difference
in what **you** eat and do.

Yy

I want you
to eat healthy and stay fit

Zz

Now I guess we've come to **Z**. Sweet **z**ucchini dreams for you and me!

Learn the ABC's of eating right,
foods that make you strong and bright.
Healthy foods for everyday,
we're ready now for work and play.

Parents to Parents

From,

Natasha & Theo Nerdelman:

1. Make the time to exercise with your children everyday.
2. Find the right exercise for your child. A child that is happy with their choice of exercise will want to continue doing it.
3. Don't forget, exercise can be as simple as a walk or a dance or even a game of tag or jump rope.
4. Share a meal with your children. It will give you the opportunity to learn about their day and be a part of their lives.
5. Turn off the TV while eating family meals.
   You will learn more about each other and eat less!!
6. Avoid drinks with lots of sugar.
   Water is the best drink to quench your thirst.
7. Follow the "Five a day rule." Eat about five servings of colorful fruits and vegetables every day.
   Remember, a serving size is about the size of your fist.
8. Balance meals with lean proteins, low fat dairy, whole grains and low saturated fat items. Avoid "Trans Fats," and foods with lots of preservatives, food additives and chemicals.
9. Serve Olive Oil with bread in place of butter. This will give you the better mono-unsaturated fat (MUFA) in place of the saturated fat.
10. Substitute olive oil or canola oil in some of your recipes.
11. The advice given here is for educational and informational purposes only. Always get your doctor's advice and permission before starting any exercise and/or nutritional program. Always seek the advice of your physician or other qualified health provider with any questions you may have regarding any medical condition.

Get Fit and Healthy The New Nerdel Way!

For Fun, Games and Information visit Nerdel and his friends at: www.nerdel.com

Nerdel is dedicated to children's health, nutrition and fitness, and most of all, everthing good for kids!

Enjoy Other Books in
The Nerdel Series of Children's Books